IMAGES
of America

C.F. MARTIN & CO.

IMAGES
of America

C.F. MARTIN & CO.

Dick Boak
Foreword by C.F. Martin IV

ARCADIA
PUBLISHING

Published by Arcadia Publishing
Charleston, South Carolina

Library of Congress Control Number: 2013949594

For all general information, please contact Arcadia Publishing:
Telephone 843-853-2070
Fax 843-853-0044
E-mail sales@arcadiapublishing.com
For customer service and orders:
Toll-Free 1-888-313-2665

Visit us on the Internet at www.arcadiapublishing.com

This book is dedicated to C. Frederick Martin III (1895–1986), who I was privileged to know. He would be most proud to read these pages to see how much his family's legacy has been extended since his passing.

CONTENTS

FOREWORD

As a teenager, I worked a number of summer jobs at Martin, became familiar with the process of crafting fine guitars, and decided pretty quickly that I wanted to be a part of it. My grandfather was the chairman of the board, and my father was the president. I spent much time with my grandfather, who relayed the stories of his life with guitars. I was enthralled and so appreciative to have him as my mentor. When he passed away in 1986, there were many in the company who thought I was too young and naive to take over the business, but I persevered and soon found myself at the helm.

I suppose I was lucky that the re-popularization of acoustic music coincided somewhat with my early tenure. Gradually, I learned the challenges of being a CEO. I was open to new ideas and technological change, but I also recognized the incredible value of the unique family-oriented culture that we were blessed with.

Looking back at our long and colorful history, I think it is quite remarkable that this company has been able to survive and prosper through innumerable shifts in musical tastes, many wars, and tremendous economic fluctuations. Why have we prospered? The people that craft the instruments over the years have shown great commitment to the integrity of the product. The designs that my great-great-great-grandfather initiated evolved without compromising the tone or quality. Musicians throughout the world have continually recognized something very special in our instruments and sought them out because they were and remain the very best tools for the job.

I have been honored to preserve and extend the legacy that was entrusted to me. The guitar is the most popular musical instrument in the world, and the company that bears my family name will continue to play a primary role in its creation for many generations to come.

—C.F. Martin IV
Chairman, C.F. Martin & Co.

ACKNOWLEDGEMENTS

Thanks to the following who have contributed so greatly to the C.F. Martin Archives: Greig Hutton, Richard Johnston, Jim Washburn, Philip Gura, John Woodland, Tom Walsh, John King, Peter Szego, Robert Shaw, Robert Goetzl, Steve Kovacik, Jim Bollman, Jacques Picard, Mark Moss, Stefan Grossman, Dan McCluskey, and the archives of the Old Town School in Chicago. Thanks to John Sterling Ruth, who has captured breathtaking photographs of Martin guitars for several decades. Thanks to C.F. Martin IV and the generations that preceded him for preserving and extending the Martin legacy. Thanks to the committed Martin employees that create these magnificent instruments. And lastly, thanks to the more than a million and a half musicians, guitar enthusiasts, and owners who have recognized Martin's quality, design, craftsmanship, and tone. A guitar is just a pretty wooden box with a neck and some wire attached until it comes alive with music. Unless otherwise noted, all images are from the C.F. Martin Archives.

INTRODUCTION

Few family businesses survive the first generation, let alone six going on seven. C.F. Martin & Co. is a unique and special family business with an alluring product and an amazing heritage. The dark, fragrant attic above the original 1859 section of the old North Street Martin factory in Nazareth, Pennsylvania, contains many relics: antique guitar molds, ancient parts, old workbenches, and scores of wooden toolboxes and crates. The Martin family saved virtually everything. One day, several dozen cartons covered in a half inch of fine Brazilian rosewood sawdust were found tucked deep under the eaves. The cartons were filled with letters and documents from the 1830s through the 1940s—each stack wrapped neatly in burlap and tied with twine—a veritable treasure trove of American musical and cultural history.

Gradually, the contents of the boxes migrated from the attic into a dedicated archive room at the newer Sycamore Street factory and headquarters. Passionate musicologists and prospective authors were given access to the records. With each round of research, the files gained acid-free preservation, coherency, and organization. In the past decade, an explosion of projects (including a yearlong exhibition of Martin guitars at the Metropolitan Museum of Art) has extended the size and scope of these precious archives. A remarkable collection of images from the dawn of photography to present day emerged. Through careful acquisition, the Martin Museum expanded its vast collection of historic instruments. Through it all, the company continued to blend old-world handcraftsmanship with modern-day technology in the manufacturing of the most revered acoustic guitars in the world. It is simply a remarkable American success story.

This book reveals the Martin story through a succession of chronological images of the many generations of the Martin family, the varied homes and factory buildings, the skilled artisans, the beautiful quill-penned sales journals, historic advertisements and posters, a smattering of special archive documents, images of the vast array of amateur and professional musicians that recognized that Martin was special, and photographs of the actual instruments as they evolved from small European parlor guitars to the full-bodied, steel-string instruments that are so immensely popular today.

Every guitar that is created goes out into the world and takes on a life of its own, absorbing the DNA and the soul of the players that extract melodies and lyrics from the vibrating tonewoods and taut strings. People do not have to be musicians to appreciate the story or the contribution that C.F. Martin & Co. has made to American culture, but it might just inspire them to become one.

One

MARKNEUKIRCHEN TO NEW YORK CITY

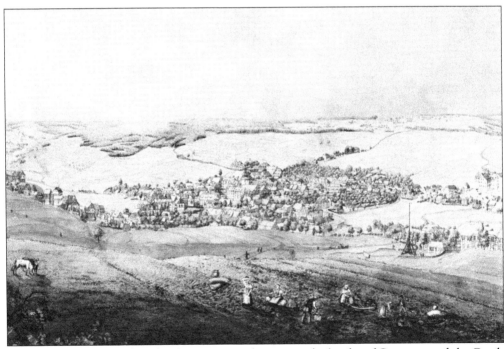

The cozy hamlet of Markneukirchen rests on what is now the border of Germany and the Czech Republic. For centuries, the town has been known as a center for musical instrument making. C.F. Martin was born here on January 31, 1796. He was the son of Johann Georg Martin, a cabinetmaker who also experimented in the making of guitars.

At the age of 15, C.F. Martin's father arranged for him to apprentice in the Viennese guitar-making shop of Johann Stauffer, a noted instrument maker of the day. C.F. learned well. He mastered all of the processes involved with the making of guitars, violins, and cellos and eventually rose to the position of shop foreman, where he gained valuable knowledge about managing a business. This guitar was made in the Stauffer shop around 1820, and it can be assumed that it was made under the supervision of C.F. Martin. After 14 years with Stauffer, C.F. met his wife-to-be, Ottilie Kühle, and went to work in her father's harp-making shop.

Shown here are Christian Frederick Martin (1796–1873) and Lucia Ottilie Kühle Martin (1803–1872).

The photographs on this page are the earliest known images of C.F. Martin Sr. and his wife, Ottilie. They were married in 1825. After the birth of their son C.F. Martin Jr., they decided to move from Vienna back to Markneukirchen, where C.F. hoped to open his own guitar-making shop. His plans were thwarted by the Violin Maker's Guild, who viewed the guitar as an inferior instrument and did not recognize his Viennese apprenticeship. After a protracted dispute, he packed up his family (that now included their young daughter Rosalie) and immigrated to America in September 1833. The family portrait above was created by Robert Goetzl, a first cousin of C.F. Martin IV.

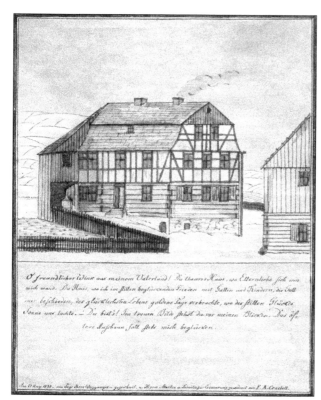

Upon the Martin's departure to America, F.A. Craslett, a close family friend from Markneukirchen, created this drawing of the Martins' German home as a memento.

After an arduous journey across the Atlantic, the Martin family arrived in New York City in November 1833, where they promptly set up shop at 196 Hudson Street, close to what is now the mouth of the Holland Tunnel. This early depiction of Five Points shows the mob violence that was prevalent in the city. It was quite a contrast for the Martins, who were accustomed to the quiet countryside of Markneukirchen. (C.F. Martin Museum; courtesy of Robert Fraker.)

Prosperous in the new world and gradually adjusting to the cultural differences, C.F. Martin Sr. posed for this portrait in the studio of Philip Zorn, a popular photographer in Philadelphia. This is the best existing image of C.F. Martin Sr.

The early guitars of C.F. Martin Sr., as seen in this exquisite presentation guitar from the New York City era, provided a template of quality, craftsmanship, and tone for the many generations that would follow.

Two

THE MOVE TO NAZARETH

Though business in New York was quite successful, the Martins were unhappy in the city. Most likely after a visit with their old friend Henry Schatz, who had preceded them in coming to America, C.F. Martin sold his property and inventory in New York and moved to Cherry Hill, Pennsylvania, in 1839, not far from Schatz's home in Millgrove. The adjacent town of Nazareth was settled by German-speaking Moravians, and the rolling hills reminded them of Markneukirchen. The Cherry Hill Hotel (shown here) still stands. It is across the street from the Martin property, which is now a small apartment complex.

The Stauffer-inspired Viennese guitar designs that C.F. Martin brought to America went through a major transformation between 1838 and 1846. Martin's implementation of X-bracing in 1843 would become the standard for nearly all acoustic guitar designs that would follow, as would all of the carefully proportioned shapes, sizes, and styles of guitars that the company would develop.

Madame Delores Nevares de Goñi was one of the most prominent and talented guitarists of her time. Her performances were widely popular throughout the Americas between 1841 and 1892. When she came through the area for a performance in Bethlehem, Pennsylvania, she visited Martin in Cherry Hill and commissioned a special larger and deeper Spanish-style instrument. Her guitar was delivered in 1843. She pronounced Martin guitars to be "superior to any instruments of the kind [she had] ever seen in this country or Europe for tone, workmanship and facility of execution!"

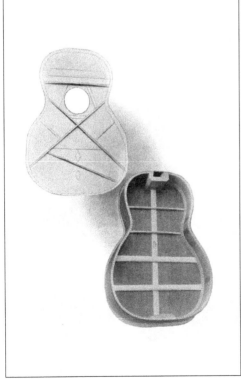

Madame de Goñi surely showed her Martin guitar to fellow musicians and fans during her extensive travels, and orders came in for many replicas of her "signature" model. Her guitar was the very first Size 1 model and the earliest X-braced guitar ever documented, supporting Martin's long-standing claim as the inventor of X-bracing, a primary innovation in the evolution of the modern American guitar. X-bracing of the top or soundboard uses less wood and distributes the stress of the strings onto the strong upper bout, or "shoulders," of the guitar, allowing the top to vibrate freely and produce great tone.

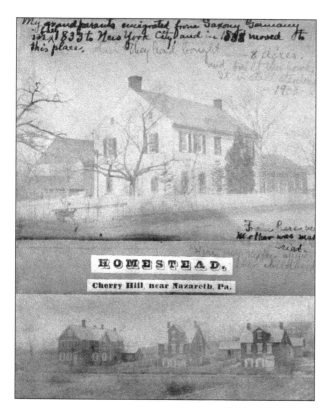

Handwritten annotations on photograph:
"My grandparents emigrated from Saxony Germany in 1833 to New York City and in 1839 moved to this place..."
"1903"

HOMESTEAD,
Cherry Hill, near Nazareth, Pa.

C.F. Martin's daughter Emilia Clara Martin married into the Ruetenik family, who kept a small journal that included many rare photographs. The top of this journal shows Martin's original Cherry Hill homestead, built in 1839. C.F. focused solely on guitar making after moving from New York. He and his family remained at this location from 1839 through 1859, when they bought a block in town, presumably to be closer to the depot from which instruments were shipped. C.F. Martin Jr. occupied the homestead on the left, C.F. Martin Sr. built the home on the right, and his first cousin, C.F. Hartmann, built the home in the center. This threesome would prove very important in the two decades that would follow.

Photograph historian and longtime daguerreotype collector Jochen Voigt of Saxony, Germany, discovered this rare c. 1850–1851 calotype of Lucia Ottilie Kühle Martin, wife of C.F. Martin Sr., taken by famous pioneer photographer Bertha Wehnert-Beckmann. Coincidentally, Wehnert-Beckmann's studio was located at 385 Broadway, a building owned by C.F. Martin and his music teacher and partner, John Coupa. The photograph was taken years after the Martins moved to Nazareth—evidence that travel was often made back to New York City to visit with friends there and to take care of business.

This very early ambrotype shows a dapper top hat–wearing musician, most likely from New York City, holding what appears to be a pre-1850 Martin guitar with a Viennese Stauffer–style headstock, but with a body shape that is more in the style of C.F. Martin Sr.'s designs. C.F. would have built this guitar personally during the time period that the guitar was transitioning from its Austro-German, Viennese, and Spanish roots to a purely American instrument. That transition was largely driven by C.F. Martin and fully developed by the late 1850s. (Courtesy of Sandy Laughner, Richmond, New Hampshire.)

CO-PARTNERSHIP.

C. F. Martin, Senior, has associated with him as Partners C. F. Martin Junior, and C. F. Hartmann, for the manufacturing of Guitars, under the firm of

C. F. MARTIN & CO.

The two new members of the firm, C. F. Martin, Junior, and C. F. Hartmann, have been employed in the above establishment over a quarter of a Century. We can therefore guarantee to our customers a first-class article, and would respectfully solicit your future patronage.

C. F. MARTIN, Sr.,
C. F. MARTIN, Jr.,
C. F. HARTMANN.

Nazareth, Penn., August, 1867.

In August 1867, C.F. Martin Sr., C.F. Martin Jr., and C.F. Hartmann formalized their business arrangement with the above copartnership agreement and the founding of C.F. Martin & Co. This notice was imprinted on the back of customer correspondence as an assurance and guarantee of the high quality of Martin guitars. C.F. Sr. was in his later years and most likely wished to put his successors firmly in place to run the business.

Martin guitars were clearly the finest instruments being made anywhere in America. As the men were off doing business or fighting wars, women represented a significant part of the musical marketplace, often entertaining houseguests in the parlors of their homes. The term parlor guitars emerged as a catchall for these smaller traditional Martin instruments. Above, two women develop their cultural appreciation of music and art.

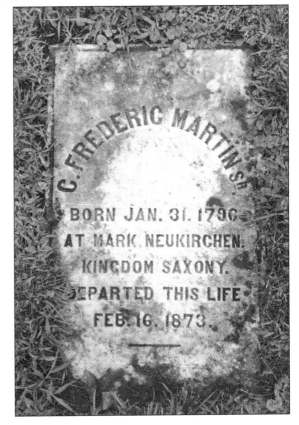

C.F. Martin Sr. suffered a mild stroke during the mid-1850s, but he remained productive on the workbench until his final days. After his death in 1873, his son C.F. Martin Jr. and first cousin C.F. Hartmann kept the business going by further standardizing the guitar models and maintaining C.A. Zoebisch & Sons in New York as an exclusive distributor of Martin guitars.

C.F. Martin Jr. (1825–1888) and Lucinda Leibfried Martin (1831–1907) are shown here. C.F. Martin Jr. saw the company through the Civil War, made the first expansion to the factory, and introduced steam-driven machinery. He was also very involved in the local community, serving as the burgess for the town and as a trustee of the Moravian Church.

This artist's rendering by Robert Goetzl depicts what the Martin homestead at the corner of Main and North Streets might have looked like after its construction in 1859. Following the completion of the home, the adjacent North Street factory was completed. A common cistern connected the basements of the two properties.

This is a side view of the Martin homestead on the corner of North and Main Streets. Though the children playing under the tree are unidentified, they are likely three of C.F. Martin Jr.'s and Lucinda's many offspring.

This is the earliest known photograph of the North Street factory. Business was apparently good, as an extension of the original brick factory and the addition of a barn-like structure were added to accommodate increased demand.

PRICE LIST

OF

C. F. MARTIN & CO'S
GUITARS.

No. 3—17	Rosewood, plain,			$30 00
" 2½—17	"	"		36 00
" 2—18	"	double bound,		37 50
" 2—20	"	Cedar neck,		42 00
" 1—21	"	"		45 00
" 2—24	"	" fancy inlaying,		50 00
" 1—26	"	inlaid with Pearl, Ivory bound,		54 00
" 2—27	"	" " "		58 50
" 0—28	"	"		60 00
" 2—30	"	" "		63 00
" 2—34	"	" "	Ivory bridge,	72 00
" 2—40	" richly "		" "	84 00
" 2—42	" " "	"	" "	90 00

No. 3.	**No. 2½.**	**No. 2.**	**No. 1.**	**No. 0.**
Small Size.	Ladies' Size.	Ladies' Size.	Large Size.	Largest Conc't Size.

All the above numbers, with Patent Head or Peg Head, and any size desired made to order.

If not specially ordered with Peg Head, Guitars with Patent Heads will be sent.

The prices above include wood case.

ALSO DEPOT FOR

Genuine "Meyer" Flutes and Piccolos,
"   "Albrecht" Flutes and Piccolos,
"Berteling" Clarionets and Flutes.
White's Chinrests.
"Rogers' Standard Banjo & Drumheads.
Tiefenbrunner Zithers.

C. A. ZOEBISCH & SON
APR 28 1888
40 MAIDEN LANE, NEW YORK

Early price lists like this one from 1888, stamped by Martin's distributor C.A. Zoebisch, were published on the backside of stationery that was used to correspond with customers. Five sizes were offered in an array of ornamented styles.

Though photography was still in its infancy and an expensive studio ordeal, there is no shortage of images of proud Martin owners, such as this guitarist from the late 1800s. This gentleman was most likely a professional, or at least a very serious player, and, as was the common practice, photographs like these were used to promote local performances or guitar instruction.

Cornellus Daniel "C.D." Schettler of Salt Lake City, Utah, was a very significant guitarist, instructor, and Martin endorsee of the 1880–1910 era. Like many of his contemporaries, he wrote for periodicals that document a vibrant community of guitarists who recognized their roots in the repertoire and techniques of Europe's great masters. The Martin 0-42 guitar he is holding is verified through correspondence in the Martin archives as being made for him in 1898.

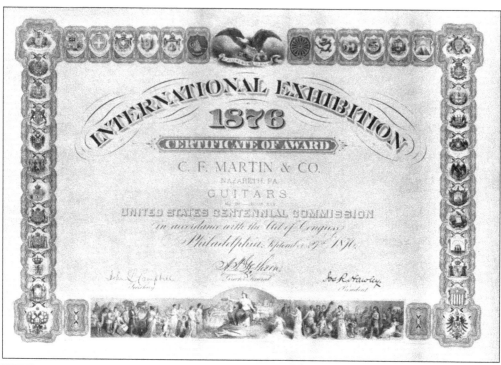

The US Centennial Commission honored Martin with the above award for "excellence in tone and good workmanship" at the 1876 International Exhibition in Philadelphia, Pennsylvania.

After the passing of his father in 1873, C.F. Martin Jr., shown at left in his later years, lived for only 15 more years, dying at the fairly young age of 63. His first child, Frank Henry Martin, was only 22 years old when C.F. Jr. died in 1888. The young son was thrust in charge of what was already the oldest and most revered guitar-making firm in the country. Many business associates might have thought the young Martin to be naive, but he proved to be anything but, bringing bold, open-minded, and innovative leadership to the company for many decades.

Shown here are Frank Henry Martin (1866–1948) and Jennie Keller Martin (1873–1972).

The extremely young Frank Henry Martin wasted little time in boldly exerting his opinion and power by terminating the exclusive arrangement with longtime distributor C.A. Zoebisch, whose conservatism was perceived to be holding the company back.

Professional musician and multi-instrumentalist George R. Stebbins is shown above around the 1890s with his banjos, guitar, mandolin, zither, and sleigh bells. The banjo and mandolin were considerably louder than the small, soft-spoken parlor guitar. To counter this, Martin guitars began to grow in size to achieve louder volume and projection.

Music could often be a rather formal affair, even in an outdoor picnic setting like this, which must have been a common scene around the turn of the 20th century.

Having established firm control over the business, Frank Henry Martin set a course for innovation and change. He was a superb craftsman, as is shown by this sign, which he cut by hand with a fine scroll saw. Although he did not attend college, he schooled himself in Latin and decided that the company needed a motto, hence "Non Multa Sed Multum" or "Not Many But Much" (quality not quantity). The sign still hangs today at the factory.

Frank and Jennie Martin had two children, both sons: C. Frederick Martin III (left) and his younger brother, Herbert Keller Martin (center). Both were groomed from an early age to be in the business.

C. F. MARTIN & CO.'S

1833–1883

CELEBRATED GUITARS.

For the past fifty years the standard and only reliable Guitar, used by all first-class Professors and Amateurs, throughout the country.

They enjoy a world wide reputation—all attempts to imitate them have failed.

They still stand this day without a rival, notwithstanding all attempts by other makers and dealers to puff up and offer inferior and unreliable Guitars.

Even the name of "MARTIN" is used in various ways to profit by its reputation.

Every "GENUINE" Martin Guitar has the maker's full name

clearly stamped twice inside the body, also on ticket on top (inside the case) stating size and number of quality.

All other Guitars of similar name offered as "MARTIN'S," not so stamped, are not "GENUINE."

NO.				PRICE EACH.
1037	3-17	Rosewood, plain,		$36 00
1038	2½-17	"		36 00
1039	2-18	" double bound,		37 50
1040	2-20	" cedar neck.		42 00
1041	1-21	" "		45 00
1042	2-24	" " fancy inlaying,		50 00
1043	1-26	" inlaid with pearl, ivory bound,		54 00
1044	2-27	" " " "		58 50
1045	0-28	" " " "		60 00
1046	2-30	" " " "		63 00
1047	2-34	" " " " ivory bridge,		72 00
1048	2-40	" richly " "		84 00
1049	2-42	" " " " screw neck,		90 00

N B.—The prices above include a wood case. If not specially ordered with peg head, Guitars with patent head will be sent.

WM. A POND & CO.
25 UNION SQUARE, NEW YORK.

Martin instruments were of such high quality that many inferior copies began to appear in the marketplace. William Pond, one of Martin's dealers, urged customers to verify the genuine article by looking for the Martin stamp on the neck and inside the body.

With the large influx of Italian immigrants in the late 1800s, the mandolin became very popular as a solo instrument, in small bands, and in larger mandolin and guitar orchestras, as evidenced in these images. Martin began producing bowlback mandolins in 1895.

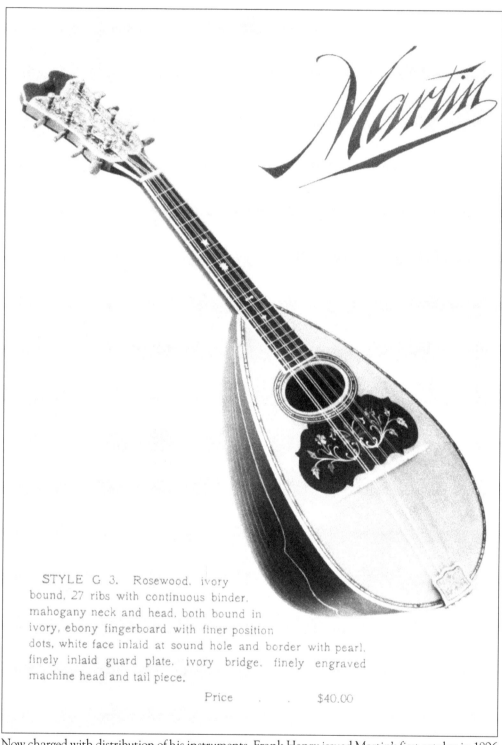

STYLE G 3. Rosewood. ivory bound, 27 ribs with continuous binder. mahogany neck and head. both bound in ivory, ebony fingerboard with finer position dots, white face inlaid at sound hole and border with pearl. finely inlaid guard plate. ivory bridge. finely engraved machine head and tail piece.

Price   .   . $40.00

Now charged with distribution of his instruments, Frank Henry issued Martin's first catalog in 1896 with the introduction of the mandolins. Mandolin players demanded the pearl embellishments that would eventually play a greater role in guitar styling.

The popularity of the mandolins spurred a New York City cottage industry of stock inlaid mandolins, pickguards, and other components, making it possible for poorly constructed mandolins to appear to be of higher quality, like this one. This is definitely not a Martin.

Martin's first Style 45 guitar appeared as a 00-sized prototype in 1902, featuring a pearl-trimmed body, a pearl-inlaid "tree of life" fingerboard, a pearl-inlaid headplate, and a pearl-inlaid pickguard, similar to bowl mandolins of the period.

This is the earliest known photograph (around 1912) of the inside of the North Street factory. Martin models continued to grow in size to compete in volume with the mandolins and banjos of the era. A batch of large 000 12-fret bodies are on the workbench.

Herbert and his older brother, C.F. III, were the first Martins to attend college. At Princeton, they had an informal duo on guitar and mandolin. They are pictured in front of the North Street factory. C.F.'s guitar had a tooled leather guitar case with a Princeton emblem on it. Both of these special Martin instruments are now part of Martin Museum collection.

William Foden (1860–1947) was a well-known guitarist and music instructor with a clientele large enough to warrant dealership status and his own exclusive line of Martin guitars called Foden Specials.

Vahdah Olcott-Bickford (above, top center) is shown with her popular virtuoso Olcott Guitar Quartet. All were loyal Martin players. Vahdah's prominence led to a high-end Style 44 signature series of guitars that were sold through Martin's largest dealer, Ditson of New York and Boston. At right, the Williamsport Westend Quartet was another all-women group from Williamsport, Pennsylvania, that featured two Martin guitars, a mandolin, and a banjo. The bearded gentleman is in the background is unidentified.

Frank Henry Martin, seen above around 1911 in the doorway with tie, stands proud with his workers outside of the North Street factory. C.F. Martin III, now a teenager, is second from the right; inlay artist Charles Anglemire is third from the right. Below, by 1920, the crew was largely the same, though Herbert Keller Martin (at far left) had joined the team.

After World War I broke out in 1917, C.F. III applied for military service but was classified 4F due to poor eyesight. Instead, he served in the Army YMCA in Blue Ridge, North Carolina, until 1919. While serving, he met his wife-to-be, Daisy Allen of Atlanta, Georgia. They were married in 1920 and returned to live in Nazareth.

MARTIN

H A W A I I A N

TARO-PATCH

F I D D L E S

—

SUPERIOR IN TONE

—

Made By

C. F. Martin & Co.

Nazareth, Pa.

Established 1833

Style 1
$15.00

Style 1
Body and neck of mahogany in an attractive dull finish. Dark rosewood fingerboard, accurately fretted; four white position marks.
    Price   :   : $15.00

Style 2
Bound front and back with white celluloid. A very effective design.
    Price   :   : $20.00

Style 3
Finely bound and trimmed with white celluloid. Extended fingerboard, seventeen frets. Pearl position marks. *Professional Model.*
    Price   :   : $30.00

The ukulele evolved from small Portuguese instruments that migrated to Hawaii on sailing ships. Early ukuleles were called taropatches and had eight strings grouped in pairs. Martin offered a number of styles. This taropatch advertisement is from 1918.

Cliff Edwards (also known as "Ukulele Ike") was a vaudeville performer and recording star who specialized in high tenor, jazzy scat singing. He is perhaps best known as the voice of Jiminy Cricket in the Walt Disney movie *Pinocchio* (1940). He was an avid ukulele player and is shown here with early film actress Bessie Love.

40

WAIKIKI TRIO

The Waikiki Trio featured a high end 12-fret 000-45 in concert with a Hawaiian slide guitar and ukulele. All three instruments appear to be Martins. Bands like this, many of which did not even include any native Hawaiians, were spurred by the incredible popularity of Hawaiian music after the Panama-Pacific International Exposition held in San Francisco in 1915.

Longtime Martin craftsman Earl Hartzell (above) sands the bent sides for Hawaiian guitars and ukuleles, which peaked in popularity in 1925, when this photograph was taken. Martin made more than 15,000 ukuleles that year—significantly more than the 2,108 guitars made.

Herbert Keller Martin was more outgoing than his older brother and perfectly suited for the task of on-the-road sales visits to Martin accounts. His success as a sales representative played a vital role in Martin's growth during the 1920s, but this all came to a tragic end when Herbert died suddenly of peritonitis in January 1927, leaving C.F. Martin III the job of assisting his father in the running of the guitar business.

Richard Konter (also known as "Ukulele Dick") is pictured here at the White House with his early 1920s Martin 1K soprano ukulele. This instrument actually accompanied Admiral Byrd's expedition and subsequent flight over the North Pole on May 9, 1926. Konter eventually donated the uke to the Martin Museum, where it is on permanent display. Along with Admiral Byrd and his complete crew, Pres. Calvin Coolidge, Thomas A. Edison, Charles Lindbergh, Gen. John J. Pershing, and a host of other dignitaries of the day signed the Konter ukulele. It is arguably one of the most valuable ukuleles in existence. The Coolidge and Lindberg signatures can be seen directly above the sound hole.

Ditson models, made by Martin, were offered in three basic sizes: small, medium, and large. The above is the small, or Baby Ditson, size, bearing a shape that is quite similar to the larger size that would be named the Dreadnought.

Martin's largest dealer between 1910 and 1930 was the Ditson Company of New York and Boston. The guitarist at right is holding a guitar made for Ditson by Martin. Ditson jumped into the ukulele and Hawaiian guitar markets early and most likely urged Martin to do the same. Although Martin began experimenting with ukulele construction as early as 1907, the designs were not refined until 1916, when production of the tiny stringed instruments exploded.

Harry L. Hunt became involved with Martin in 1893 while working for the William A. Pond music store in New York City. He left to head up the musical instrument department of Ditson's impressive New York City location. In 1916, his collaboration with Frank Henry Martin and Martin shop foreman John Deichman led to the design and naming of the famous Martin Dreadnought model.

The period between the two world wars was a time of great innovation, experimentation, and exceptional handcraftsmanship at Martin that has come to be called the Golden Era. Many ideas were successful and many were not, but there was no reticence to try bold new ideas. This unusual eight-string Hawaiian-style Octachorda was ordered by Ditson's Harry Hunt in 1925, but an onslaught of ukulele orders deferred the prototype's completion until 1930 as the Great Depression hit. It was never delivered and has remained in the Martin collection ever since.

Three

THE GOLDEN ERA

Longtime employee
George Hineline of
Tatamy, Pennsylvania,
works on a 14-fret
000-18 in the Filling
Department at
the North Street
factory. (Courtesy
of Kevin Sandt.)

Ditson's Harry L. Hunt, Frank Henry Martin, and his son C.F. Martin III were all history buffs. When it came time to introduce what would be the largest new guitar model to date, they named it after the largest in a class of British battleships: the Dreadnought.

Longtime Martin employee and shop foreman John Deichman was an avid guitarist and expert guitar maker. He played a significant role, together with Harry Hunt of Ditson and Frank Henry Martin, in the collaborative original development of the Dreadnought guitar. Originally a 12-fret design, it evolved in the early 1930s into a 14-fret model that would eventually overtake the nation to become the most popular musical instrument worldwide.

The 12-fret Dreadnought, originally produced by Martin exclusively for the Ditson Company of New York and Boston, was referred to as a bass guitar because of its strong, low-end response. It was strung with elevated steel strings and played in the Hawaiian style with a slide. It was eventually produced for standard play, as evidenced by this 1929 Ditson 111 model, but the Great Depression saw the bankruptcy of Ditson in 1931, leaving the door open for Martin to produce the Dreadnought under its own name.

Railroad man Jimmie Rodgers was known as the "Singing Brakeman," "Blue Yodeler," and subsequently the "Father of Country Music." In his travels around the country, he gathered diverse musical influences and combined them into a 12-bar format that would heavily influence the emerging American folk, country, and blues styles. His priceless Blue Yodel 000-45 Martin guitar, made in 1927, is on display at the Jimmie Rodgers Museum in Meridian, Mississippi.

Jimmie Rodgers hired an itinerant sign painter to embellish the back of his guitar with "thanks." After every song, he would flip his guitar around to show his appreciation for the delighted crowds that would gather at railroad stops to hear him play.

In 1996, Martin master craftsman Dale Eckhart accompanied Dick Boak to Meridian, Mississippi, to personally inspect and measure the original Jimmie Rodgers guitar for a special 000-45 limited edition model. The valuable guitar was stored overnight in an on-site bank vault.

Pictured here is a 1926 picnic at Bushkill Park. From left to are (first row) unidentified wives and seated children; (second row) five unidentified, William Miller, Charles Roth, Clarence Metz, Emery Trach, Floyd Young, Floyd Oberly, Harold Hearn, Clayton Reese, George Stettler, Floyd Morris, Archie Goodhart, Lester Heffelfinger, Clark Rash, Steward Metz, and seven unidentified; (third row) George Hineline, David Mack, John Deichman, Edgar Barrall, Arlington Peters, Clement Fehr, Steward Metz, Edgar Bartholomew, Clinton Hahn, George Kriedler, Elmer Werkheiser, three unidentified children, Harry Troxell, Norman Garr, Robert Troxell, Norman Milheim, and Ezra Gum; (fourth row) Mark Parseghian, Arling Nicholas, Grant Remaley, Howard Bartholomew, Lester Werkheiser, Chester Gower, Roy Hildenbrandt, Elwood Hahn, C. Frederick Martin, unidentified, Charles Savitz, Herbert Martin, Charles Nicholas, Henry Beck, Russell Werkheiser, Morgan Hineline, Jim Rice, and Steward Berger.

Commemorating the 100th anniversary of C.F. Martin's 1833 arrival in America, Martin employees paraded the town aboard a decorated truck.

At Martin's 100th anniversary celebration, the enthusiastic paraders disembarked from their truck and joined in an impromptu performance on guitar, mandolin, and ukulele.

For the 200th anniversary of the town of Nazareth (1740–1940), residents and businesses pulled out all of the stops. Martin joined in with a celebratory float. The two children on the float are Frank Herbert Martin and his sister Pamela Martin.

Perry Bechtel of Atlanta, Georgia, was perhaps the greatest banjo player in America, but as the banjo began to wane in popularity in the late 1920s, Perry was being increasingly called upon to perform with the guitar. He was used to being able to play all the way up the neck on his plectrum banjo, and in 1930, he asked Martin whether a guitar could be made with 15 frets clear of the body, as opposed to the standard 12-fret models. Martin laid it out on paper and responded that they could make him a 14-fret version. Hence, the Orchestra Model was born. Though it took a few years to catch on, the longer-scale Orchestra Model had a great tone, and the 14-fret neck design migrated quickly to other Martin styles and sizes.

The 14-fret Orchestra Model, with its squared-off shoulders, allowed for greater access to the upper registers of the guitar, and the slightly longer string length gave it versatility for both finger-style and strummed techniques. This is a top-of-the-line OM-45 from 1933.

Most likely in response to the success that the Gibson Guitar Company was having with their archtop models, Martin introduced its own C Series, F Series, and R Series archtops in 1931, mostly based upon existing Martin sizes and construction methods. Though a surprising number were sold, these models were discontinued in 1942, but not before actor James Cagney bought one to play between filming sessions on a movie set.

Always willing to address a new market, Frank Henry Martin dabbled in banjos with the introduction of this tenor model in 1923, which appealed to the marching string-band market. Only 96 of these were made before their discontinuation in 1926.

Singing cowboys like Roy Rogers (above) and Gene Autry embraced the new more modern Orchestra Model guitars that were better for stage and recording use. Roy is playing his OM-45 Deluxe that recently sold at a Christie's auction for more that $600,000.

Martin expanded the North Street factory in 1925 and 1926 to accommodate the huge demand for ukuleles. By the early 1930s, when this photograph was taken, North Street had maximized the footprint of the property. The street was finally paved but was still without sidewalks.

Leonard Zapf Jr. of Zapf's Music in Philadelphia, Pennsylvania, visited Martin around 1940 to conduct some business, as Zapf's was an important dealership. By this time, the sidewalks and curbing had finally been added.

Radio, television, and movie star Gene Autry owned many beautiful high-end Martin instruments throughout his long career, but perhaps his most famous guitar is the D-45 Dreadnought that was specially made for him in 1933, with his name prominently inlaid in mother of pearl. This is the very first top-of-the-line D-45 ever made.

Martin has been involved in string distribution from the onset. This very rare 1938 counter display from the Martin Archives lights up, and the "Martin" letters bubble up in an orange glow from heated glass tubes.

Because of the Hawaiian slide guitar craze and the popularity of mandolins, steel strings gained popularity in the early 1900s. By 1922, Martin began offering steel strings as stock on the majority of models. Early on, Martin strings were made up by piano wire vendors such as Mapes, then packaged and distributed by Martin to primarily US dealerships.

Music stores that were fortunate enough to have the Martin line often made lavish displays of Martin instruments, as seen above at Kutz Music Store in Pittsburg, Kansas, and below at Lyon and Healy in Chicago, Illinois.

Frank Henry Martin was an avid photographer and loved to travel. With a grown son helping to run the business, he was afforded the time for many vacation trips. Here he is at Miami Beach on New Year's Day 1941, enjoying the sunshine in full suit and tie.

Three generations of Martins are seen outside of the North Street factory around 1940; C.F. Martin III (left) is with his son Frank Herbert Martin (center) and Frank Henry Martin (right).

C.F. Martin III (right) was interviewed live on NBC Radio by Mike Wallace and Mike's cohost/wife, Buff Cobb, in 1951. This happened most likely at the Chicago NAMM Show for musical instruments, and it can be assumed that the topic was the company's great history and success.

Frank Henry Martin (1866–1948) is seen here in later years with his wife, Jennie Keller Martin.

A proud C.F. Martin III samples a 00-18G nylon-string model inside the ground floor entrance of North Street. Note the boxed ukuleles ready on the shelves to the left.

Clark Rash and Clayton Reece take a break inside the ground floor entrance to the North Street factory, where the guitars, mandolins, and ukuleles were strung, tuned, cased, and packed for shipment to Martin dealers.

The binding area at North Street was on the upper floor of the 1925–1926 expanded wing of the factory. The natural light was perfect for guitar assembly.

North Street's machining area was located on the second floor of the 1925–1926 expanded wing. Here, the large Tannewitz band saw was used to cut neck billets from three-inch-thick planks of mahogany. The spindle-shaping machine is on the right.

Fitting the neck to the body's dovetail joint perfectly is perhaps the most difficult job in the making of a Martin guitar. Here, the neck of a 00-17 is in its final fit before hide gluing.

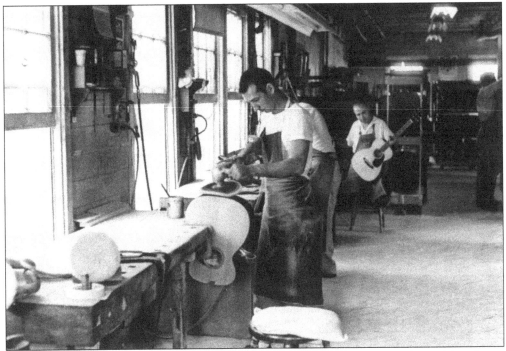

Ken Smith Jr. started as a young man at North Street in the polishing area and transitioned over to the new Sycamore Street facility in 1964, where he remained for his entire working life. Prior to his retirement in 1993, Ken worked in the repair department.

This area of the 1925–1926 expanded wing was set aside for instrument repair. This unidentified worker appears to be checking the internal bracing with an inspection mirror.

This is the second-floor south wall of the 1925–1926 expanded wing in 1949. The top and back gluing wheel is on the left, and parts are racked for seasoning in the ceiling.

Another view of the second-floor south wall of the 1925–1926 expansion shows a worker in the body assembly department installing endpiece inlays on ukuleles.

This 1949 view of the body assembly area shows a predominance of the more affordable mahogany 00 and 000-18 bodies, popular after the war for their tone and price.

Milt Hess Sr. had a long career with Martin. He is shown here in 1963 bending ukulele sides over the hot iron at the North Street factory. In 1964, North Street production was moved to Sycamore Street.

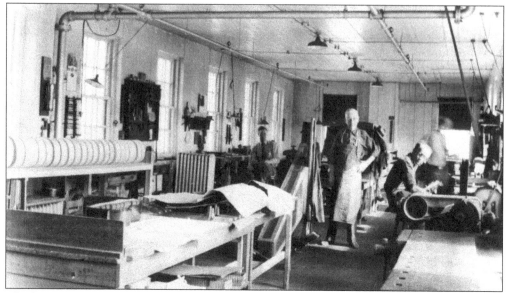

Charlie "Doc" Savitz (standing center) was the foreman of the area on North Street's second floor where fingerboards were glued to the necks, necks were fit to the body, frets were hammered in, and position dots were inlaid.

As the Dreadnought took off, demand for Martin quality and tone led to an increase in the number of craftsman needed to get the job done. D-28 bodies are on the shop cart.

Shortly after leaving Bill Monroe's bluegrass band in 1948, Lester Flatt enlisted Earl Scruggs to form the Foggy Mountain Boys, which became one of the premier bluegrass bands of all time. "Foggy Mountain Breakdown" was a popular hit on the radio and on the stage of the Grand Ole Opry. Lester's famous D-28 was modified with inlay by soon-to-become Martin historian Mike Longworth.

Though traditional bluegrass and country bands gathered around a single microphone, the demands of stage performing together with the rising popularity of electric guitars enticed Martin to introduce electrified models with installed Rowe DeArmond pickups. Traditional Martin players must have been appalled by the drilled holes and routed pockets on what were otherwise pristine acoustic Martins. The D-18E, introduced in 1960, was only available for a year, though the D-28E had a slightly longer life.

With 11 singles reaching number one on the country charts, Hank Williams had a huge impact and influence upon American music. He played an assortment of Martin D-18 and D-28 Dreadnoughts up until his tragic death in 1953 at the young age of 30.

C.F. Martin III (center) must have been awfully proud to join up with Dave Guard (left), Bob Shane (second from left), and Nick Reynolds (right) of the Kingston Trio at Princeton University on November 5, 1960. The short fellow with the cap is their upright bass player, David "Buckwheat" Wheat. Martin was as proud a graduate of Princeton as one could ever find, and the Kingston Trio's huge popularity certainly helped to sell a lot of Martin guitars.

Crooner Perry Como (left) and comedian George Gobel donned their Martin guitars for a performance on the *Perry Como Show* in January 1961.

The Kingston Trio made music accessible to a generation of college students that went out and bought Martin guitars and Vega banjos. Few other groups had such an impact upon Martin sales. As the folk-era boom was ushered in, customers had to wait up to four years to get a D-28. After much prodding, Frank Herbert Martin was successful in convincing his father, C.F. Martin III, to break ground on a new, more modern factory.

Four

SYCAMORE STREET

Most likely because of the huge backlog of orders, Frank Herbert Martin eventually was able to convince his reticent and traditional father, C.F. Martin III, to build a more modern factory. At the peak of the folk boom in 1963, architects Fulmer and Bowers from Princeton, New Jersey, completed their vision for the new Sycamore Street Martin facility. After more than 100 years, the North Street plant would cease to be the place where Martin guitars were made.

On a dreary, snow-covered day, members of the Nazareth Association of Industrial Development Authority joined C.F. Martin III (second from right) for the ground breaking.

Coincidentally, the Sycamore Street facility was built on a plot that had once been part of C.F. Martin Sr.'s Cherry Hill property. The building was completed and final preparations were made for a grand opening in the early autumn of 1964.

On September 27, 1964, Martin opened the doors of the new factory to employees, their families, and local residents for an official grand celebration.

The new factory provided better lighting and greater space all on one level, as opposed to the many floors of North Street. This allowed for a much more efficient layout in what C.F. Martin III liked to call "an assembly line of handcraftsmanship."

Tom Paxton made a name for himself in the early 1960s Greenwich Village folk scene with songs like "The Last Thing On My Mind." When the grand opening of the new factory was being planned in 1964, Frank Martin invited Paxton to entertain from the loading platform of the new plant.

Like Tom Paxton, Judy Collins was basking in the folk limelight in 1964 with her third album that featured songs of folk compatriots like Bob Dylan and Pete Seeger. She joined Paxton in a performance from the loading platform. Appropriately, both Tom and Judy returned to Martin on October 25, 2006, for the grand reopening of the new museum and visitor center.

Phil Moll (right) worked for decades in the body assembly area and was foreman of the department in his later years. It appears he is gluing the rear block for an A mandolin in this image.

Russ Lilly, another longtime employee, was the foreman of the machine room that was charged with processing wood into guitar parts. This included joining and seasoning tops, backs, and sides into special racks—a far cry from the ceiling racks at North Street.

When the new factory was completed in 1964, Frank Herbert Martin held the position of director of sales while his father retained the positions of president and chairman of the board. New modern furniture replaced the old rolltop desk.

Office manager Joan Johnson (left) with her husband, Bob Johnson (standing), are talking to the typist and a visitor. Bob was the vice president and was responsible for the introduction of the D-35—Martin's bold, three-piece-back model introduced in 1965. C.F. III is seated in the corner office in the background.

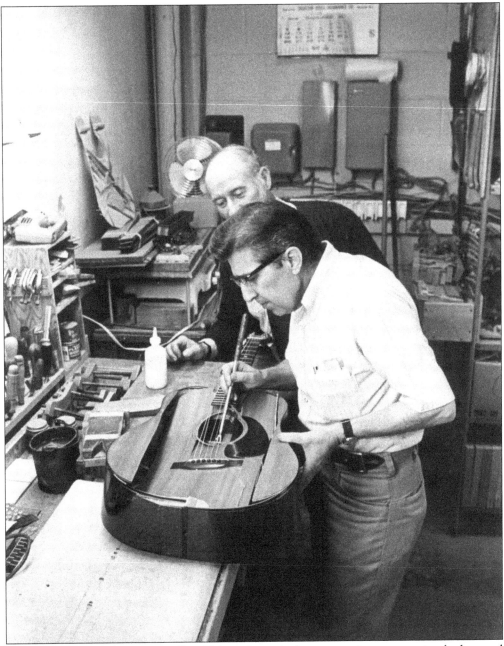

Lester Davidson and Jim Rampulla of Martin's repair department inspect a seriously damaged Martin D-18 in 1965. Believe it or not, even guitars in this condition could be rebuilt, though this one would have surely needed a new soundboard.

Earl Remaly began working at the North Street factory as a teenager in the late 1940s. He was a seasoned guitar expert by the time the move to Sycamore Street was made. Here, he is inspecting a batch of F Series electric guitars that were offered between 1961 and 1965.

Martin GT Electric guitars were offered between 1965 and 1967 with double cutaways, DeArmond pickups, and unusual scalloped headstocks. A line of amplifiers made for Martin by the Allen Organ Co. of Macungie, Pennsylvania, was introduced as well. Martin board member Frank Schroeder of Schroeder Design in Philadelphia, who did all of Martin's creative work during this era, took this photograph, dubbed "The Martin Girls," for an advertisement.

Prior to departing for India, Beatles members Paul McCartney and John Lennon bought matching Martin D-28s, and while George Harrison was busy meditating with the Maharishi, they wrote 42 songs that would become *The White Album*, *Let It Be*, and *Abbey Road*. (Photograph by Paul Saltzman; all rights reserved.)

While there were several other companies making acoustic guitars, Martin dominated the market in both quality and quantity. Because so many musicians played Martin instruments voluntarily, there was little interest in endorsement. The list of Martin players has always read like a who's who of American musical culture. At left is Elizabeth Cotton—famous for her finger-style anthem "Freight Train"—with her Martin 00-18. Although she was left handed, she learned to play a right-handed guitar upside down.

Bobby Joe Fenster puts down the world

Martin had a long-standing policy of not dealing directly with artists and there was no formalized endorsement program, as with many of the other guitar manufacturers. Frank Martin poked fun at artist endorsees by creating superhero Bobby Joe Fenster, a fictitious Martin player complete with cape and toting a 12-fret D-28S model.

MARTIN GUITAR

Martin's simple yet iconic "hand logo" made an indelible impression upon the guitarists of the 1960s and 1970s. Used on catalogs, posters, company literature, and letterhead, the hand logo gave a consistent, recognizable style to the growing company brand.

The Martin Guitar still handmade

Martin's advertising strategy, driven by Frank Schroeder of Schroeder Design, was focused on a simple message: Martin guitars are still handmade. The advertisements were often accompanied by posters that were steeped in craftsmanship and class.

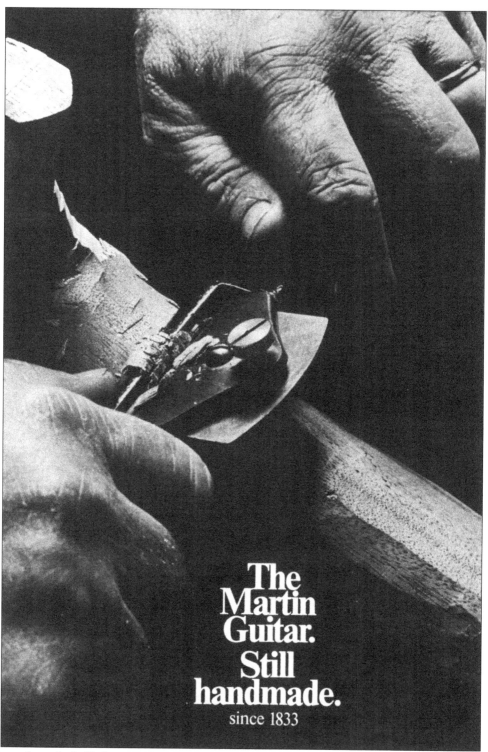

The Martin Guitar. Still handmade.
since 1833

Apart from the bold photographic imagery of handcraftsmanship, Frank Schroeder was an expert at creating unique and classy typography for Martin advertisements and literature.

Many Martin employees were appropriately adept musicians, as shown in this photograph that ran as an advertisement with the headline "We Not Only Make 'Em—We Play 'Em!"

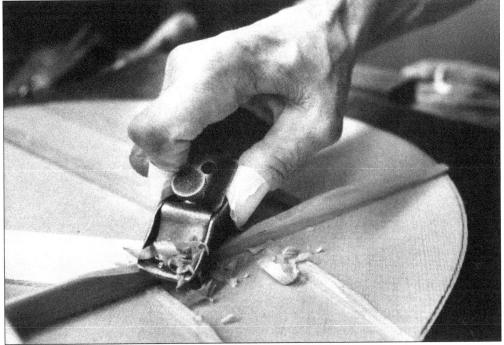

The guitar-making environment at Martin provided numerous engaging visual images for hands-on promotion, like the hand scalloping of the top braces with a finger plane.

Meet Mike

This is Mike Longworth,
he works for us
and he works for you.

You may have already met Mike
at the many folk festivals
and concerts that he has attended
all over America.

Mike won't try to sell you a guitar
or a banjo or anything, but he will
lend you his ear and any advice you
may need concerning the care of
your guitar, and if you want to
just talk music that's fine too.

Look Mike up, he's another way
we can continue to let you know
we care.

Martin Guitars

Makers of fine guitars since 1833

Inlay expert Mike Longworth was hired in 1968 to assist Martin in the reintroduction of the top-of-the-line D-45. Perhaps his greatest contribution to the company was his authorship of the book *Martin Guitars: A History*, a project that began to organize the vast archives that the Martin family had kept faithfully through the years.

The Martin Archives, one of the most complete collections of American culture and business, contains photographs, journals, letters, artifacts, draftings, log books, and even cancelled checks from the 1830s, as pictured above.

Darco was Martin's primary source for strings, and in 1970, Frank Martin purchased the Darco Musical String Company of Long Island City, New York, from the D'Addario family. From left to right are Albert Morante, Gino Burrelli, John D'Addario Jr., and John D'Addario Sr.

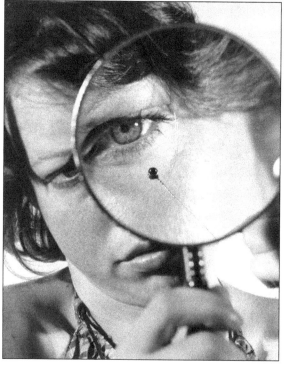

A Darco worker carefully inspects the quality of a ball-ended bronze wound string.

Darco workers at the Long Island City facility apply the bronze wrapping to the silvered steel core wire on winding machines specially developed for the purpose. In 1985, the manufacturing of strings would be moved from Long Island City to Nazareth.

The top-of-the-line Martin Marquis strings featured silk wrapping to protect the bridge.

Lon Werner worked in quality control for many years before managing the string division and the repair department. This photograph was taken in final inspection in 1972.

Eddie Mast (left) was a professional basketball player who came to the Lehigh Valley to play for the Allentown Jets—a team that Frank Martin owned and coached. Frank hired Eddie, who became an expert in exotic wood importation until his passing in 1994.

The Sawmill, Inc., was built in 1975 on the south side of the Sycamore Street facility to cut logs of mahogany and rosewood, but as these species became difficult to acquire, the mill began importing alternate exotic species for sale to the premium woodworking market.

Bill Hall, an expert sawyer from a New Hampshire sawmill operation, was hired in 1975 to run Martin's Brenta band mill, which could accommodate large logs up to 46 inches in diameter. A huge bubinga log presented a different challenge for Bill. This 24-foot-long log, weighing 42,000 pounds, needed to be cut into 8-foot lengths before the sections were sawed to fit on the mill's carriage.

Given that there was a large gap between the average selling price of an acoustic guitar and the lowest price of a Martin, Frank Martin began importing a more entry-level line of instruments from Japan under the Sigma brand. These were final inspected for quality in Nazareth. As the standard of living rose in Japan, Sigma manufacturing moved to other countries in the Pacific Rim. The brand was discontinued and eventually sold in 2010.

Like many Martin workers, Frank Kern was a seasoned craftsman. As the 1980s came to a close, many of the seasoned employees that had been hired after World War II began to retire, and it became increasingly important to document their methods and train new employees.

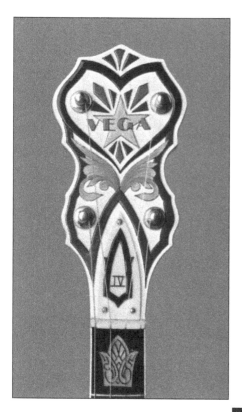

Frank Martin acquired the prestigious Vega Banjo Company of Boston in 1970 and produced several price ranges of tenor, plectrum, and five-string banjos of high quality. In addition, Martin began producing Vega-branded guitars at the Egmond factory in the Netherlands. The high cost of manufacturing coupled with relatively low sales and profitability led to the sale of the Vega brand to Galaxy Trading Company in 1979. Subsequently, Deering Banjo Company of Spring Valley, California, noticed that Galaxy had allowed the Vega trademark to lapse. Deering was successful in registering it and now owns the Vega brand.

In 1973, Frank Martin acquired the Levin brand of instruments from Herman Carlson Levin. The large manufacturing facility in Gothenburg, Sweden, proved to be difficult for Martin to manage from such a distance. Martin closed the factory in 1981.

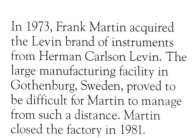

Originally founded by jazz drummer Bobby Grauso (right) and composite materials expert John Marina in 1966, the Fibes Drum Company was bought by Frank Martin in the early 1970s. Manufacturing was set up in Easton, Pennsylvania. A specialty was clear Plexiglas drum shells, but an assortment of chrome and wood laminate shells were also made. After about 10 years, low prioritization and limited sales saw the sale of the brand and inventory. Another acquisition, Manos Woods, made drumsticks under the Fibes name, but that too was a distraction from Martin's core guitar-making business.

Frank Martin's attempts to build a musical conglomerate were, with the exception of the purchase of the Darco String Company, failures. The Goya brand passed through many owners before ending up in Martin's hands as part of the Levin brand acquisition. Originally made in Sweden, their manufacture moved to South Korea. Goya guitars were offered as entry-level instruments through Martin's telemarketing efforts of the 1980s and 1990s. The Goya brand was sold to Goya Foods in 1999 as brand consolidation.

After Frank Herbert Martin left the business in 1982, his father mentored young Chris Martin IV on the preservation of quality, the family-oriented company culture, and the legacy of the company that would soon become his to manage.

C.F. Martin III loved to be one of the gang, as shown in this photograph from an employee picnic at the local Bushkill Park in 1984. He liked to be called Fred, though virtually everyone called him Mr. Martin out of great respect.

C.F. Martin III passed away in June 1986 at the age of 92. He loved guitars and the associated business, and he was firmly committed to the community and the workers that he employed. He came to work daily, visited the varied workbenches in his regular walks through the shop, and knew everyone on a first name basis. He saw the company through prosperous and hard times. His great legacy was the preservation of the integrity and quality of the guitars he so loved.

After C.F. Martin III's passing, there was a short transition before the board of directors appointed Chris Martin as chairman. He was 30 years old at the time. C. Hugh "Tigger" Bloom (left) retained the presidency position until his retirement in 1994.

The binding or edging on a guitar seals the end grain, protects the instrument from dents, and adds the primary styling. Elaine Dillard worked at Martin for 26 years and excelled in the binding department before moving to the pearl inlay area.

An expert at many critical jobs like dovetail neck fitting and ukulele construction, longtime employee Willard "Buddy" Silvius carves a neck with a drawknife.

Five

A LASTING LEGACY

James Trach Sr., who worked for several decades in the final inspection and repair departments, gives a primer in stringing and setup to young CEO Chris Martin in 1989. Chris faced many challenges. A workforce steeped in tradition was not immediately receptive to change and newer competitive technologies, but Chris managed to implement fresh ideas and grow the company exponentially while preserving a family business atmosphere and culture.

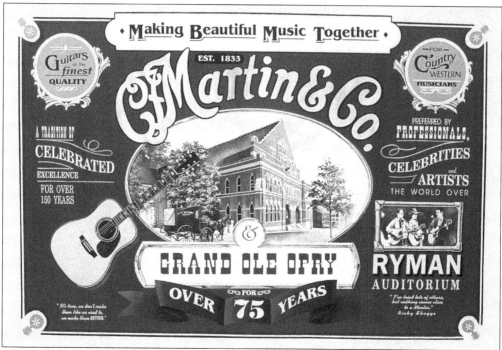

Martin was a primary sponsor of the Opryland USA theme park outside of Nashville from 1976 until the park's closing in 1997. This sign greeted visitors as they approached the Martin Guitar's Country and Bluegrass Theatre, an outdoor stage that featured Russ and Becky Jeffers' band Smokey Mountain Sunshine, as well as Opry mainstays like Porter Wagoner, Little Jimmy Dickens, Roy Acuff, Bill Anderson, Jeannie Pruitt, and Charlie Collins.

Shown here from left to right are Dan Kelly, Becky Jeffers, Russ Jeffers, Charlie Collins, and Larry McNeely at the Martin Guitar's Country and Bluegrass Theatre, Opryland USA, in Nashville, Tennessee.

Anticipating the 250th anniversary celebration (1840–1990) of Nazareth, Pennsylvania, Martin employees applied their craftsmanship to the creation of a colossal 9:1 scale Martin guitar that served as an impressive float. The giant guitar is now on display in the factory.

Chris Martin joined in the fun with dozens of employees that all dressed in 1840s attire and boarded the float for Nazareth's 250th anniversary parade.

Around the time that the Backpacker guitar was first introduced, a call came in from NASA mission specialist Pierre Thuot. He was in a band called Quantum Force and wanted to be the first to play a guitar aboard the space shuttle. Bob McNally, inventor of the Backpacker, made a specially sized "Space Guitar" that would fit in the shuttle storage compartment. The advertisement above commemorated the launch.

NASA mission specialist Pierre Thuot performed weightless from outer space aboard the STS-62 *Columbia* space shuttle in March 1994 with the miniature Backpacker Space Guitar. His fellow astronauts kidded him about his performance, which was televised live on the *Today Show*.

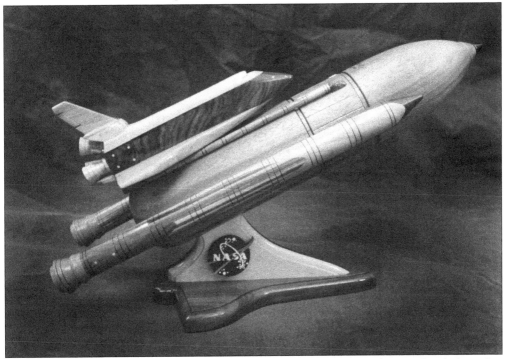

NASA employee and expert woodworker Scott Phillips commemorated many shuttle launches with beautiful models like this one from the Martin Museum, made with mahogany, rosewood, and ebony tonewoods from Martin production.

With the open-minded leadership of Chris Martin, Nazareth guitar making thrived and business grew, requiring many successive expansions of the factory. This is the expanded binding area at Sycamore Street in 2005.

While Chris Martin managed the business as CEO and chairman, Robert C. "Bob" Hoch, who joined the company in 1974 as a CPA, assumed the presidency of the company in the mid-1990s. A significant initiative of Hoch's was Momex, Martin's maquiladora in Mexico that started with string manufacture and evolved to include the affordable Backpacker, Little Martin, 1 Series, and Road Series instruments. Martin's Mexican operation in Navojoa serves as a model for successful NAFTA business collaborations. After his retirement in 2003, Bob served on Martin's board of directors for many years.

After the success of string and Backpacker manufacturing in Navojoa, Mexico, Martin expanded the operation with a high pressure laminate X Series and solid wood 1 Series guitar production to address the more affordably priced guitar market. Here, a Momex employee samples a 000 model in the final inspection area of the plant.

After the ball ending and the application of brass or phosphor bronze wrapping, strings are treated and hung to dry in advance of envelope insertion and final packaging.

A masterful guitarist and performer, David Bromberg played a significant role in the development of the 0000 or M-sized guitars that evolved from the largest of the F-hole archtop Martins. Several of these instruments were retrofitted with flat tops in the 1970s. The M models are especially prized onstage and in the studio since the notes resound without the associated overtones than can cause feedback through microphones and sound systems.

Sting's commitment to rainforest protection led to the development of three different models made with responsibly harvested tonewoods. Martin has him to thank for an evolving line of Certified and Sustainable Wood models that will surely play a significant role in the future of instrument making.

Early in her career, Joan Baez fell in love with a 1929 0-45 Martin guitar, and she has played it ever since. In 1998, Martin honored Joan and her beautiful vintage guitar with the 0-45JB Signature Edition. These smaller, traditional 12-fret guitars have a sweetness and strength of tone that belies their size.

Mark Knopfler's guitar artistry is revered for his unique technique and touch. As the front man for Dire Straits and a prolific solo artist, his songwriting has provided a canvas for exploring a wide array of delicate tones. In 2001, Martin introduced the HD-40MK Mark Knopfler Dreadnought that Mark dubbed "the Strummer." In 2006, a follow-up 000-40S Knopfler edition dubbed "the Picker" rounded out his Martin arsenal.

The Martin Museum and Visitors Center was completed in 2005 with raving reviews from the many thousands of visitors that make the trip to "Guitar Mecca" each year. The museum tells

the story of the Martin family, the evolution of the acoustic guitar, and the innumerable Martin artists that have contributed to American music and culture.

C.F. Martin Sr.'s first location in America was 196 Hudson Street in the Tribeca section of Manhattan, near the mouth of the Holland Tunnel. David Yurman, who occupies the building at that address, collaborated with Tribeca Native and Trinity Real Estate to create a special plaque to commemorate C.F. Martin's historical presence. The plaque was unveiled on November 7, 2008—almost 175 years to the day when C.F. Martin arrived in New York City.

Seen here at the dedication of the bronze C.F. Martin plaque at Hudson Street are, from left to right, Dick Boak, Walter Chefitz of David Yurman Jewelry, Nicole Bartelme of Tribeca Native, Chris Martin, and Tom Cancelliere, director of Trinity Property Management.

The Martin's Nazareth homestead, built in 1859 at the corner of North and Main Streets, served as the home for several generations of the family. It is still owned by Martin but currently houses the Nazareth Area Chamber of Commerce.

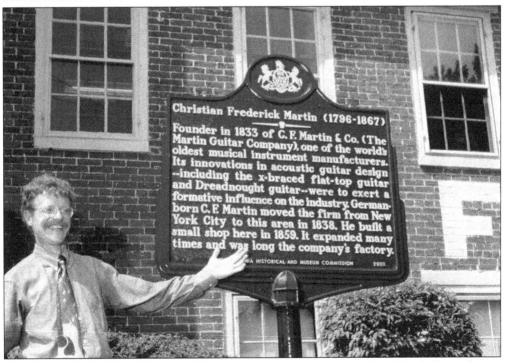

The Pennsylvania Historical and Museum Commission commemorated the North Street factory and the achievements of C.F. Martin Sr. with a historical marker in 2000.

Hawaii's beloved singer and ukulele master Israel Kamakawiwo'ole, better known as "IZ," helped repopularize the ukulele and Hawaiian music from the 1970s through the 1990s with his hit medley "Over The Rainbow/ What A Wonderful World." IZ passed away in 1997, but his legacy lives on. He is pictured with his Martin ukulele that provided the inspiration for a 2012 commemorative edition of IZ 1T Tenor ukuleles.

Scott Chinery loved guitars and emerged in the 1980s and 1990s as one of the most significant instrument collectors in America. In the early 1990s, he commissioned Martin to make the Goliath guitar—a very large Larson Bros.–inspired guitar with a 19-inch span across the widest part of the body. This instrument is perhaps one of the rarest Martin guitars ever made.

John Mayer introduced a fresh new acoustic sound with his first album *Room For Squares* in 2001. Since then, he has continually proven his staying power and musicianship. A loyal Martin player from the start, he has been honored with four unique signature editions. He is shown above in Laurel Canyon in 2011 with his 00-45SC Stagecoach Edition, named because small parlor guitars like this were delivered by stagecoach.

Martin serial numbers are sequential, so when a significant number is on the horizon, something very special is called for. This is serial number 1,000,000, made in 2004.

The unprecedented inlay for the millionth guitar combined Martin's Style 45 craftsmanship with the incredible inlay artistry of Larry Robinson. It took two years to complete.

The incredible growth in demand for Martin guitars saw the completion of serial number 1,500,000 in 2011, just six years after the one-millionth guitar. DaVinci Unplugged was the chosen theme for this milestone. The talents of inlay artist Harvey Leach, scrimshaw engraver Bob Hergert, and metal artist Tira Mitchell combined with Martin's impeccable construction to create this museum masterpiece. Every shade and detail is a separate piece of selected inlay.

A painstakingly inlaid depiction of *The Last Supper* graces the pickguard of the DaVinci Unplugged guitar. Scrimshaw engravings from DaVinci's journals adorn the bridge.

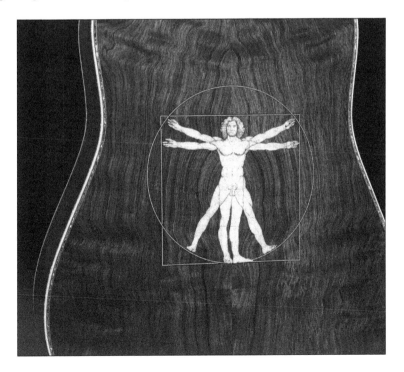

DaVinci's *Vitruvian Man* is inlaid and scrimshaw engraved on the back of serial number 1,500,000. The illustration bears a remarkable similarity to Martin X-bracing.

Lehigh Valley's popular guitarist Craig Thatcher began working as a Martin artist and clinician in 2007, traveling around the world while performing and demonstrating new models, especially the acoustic-electric Performing Artist and Retro Series guitars.

Eric Clapton's virtuosity and popularity as a guitarist are unmatched. From the beginning of his career, he has been drawn to Martin guitars, especially the smaller-bodied 000 models that have enhanced his acoustic expressiveness. His *MTV Unplugged* performance in 1992 spurred great interest in the Martin guitars he was playing. This resulted in an unprecedented collaboration with Clapton that has spanned two decades and created more than 10 immensely popular signature editions. In fact, Clapton is responsible for the repopularization of the 000-size guitar. With more than 20,000 Martin guitars bearing his name, the 000 guitar has become synonymous with his tone and playing style.

While reading a copy Martin's magazine, the *Sounding Board*, Eric Clapton noticed an article about the masterpiece leather cover that Al Shelton had created for the Martin Museum. Following in the tradition of Elvis Presley, Rick Nelson, Hank Snow, and many others, Clapton commissioned his own version by leather artist Chuck Smith. This is undeniably the most beautiful and ornate leather artistry ever created for a guitar.

Completed in December 2005, the Martin Museum and Visitors Center replaced the existing facade at Sycamore Street with a replication of the North Street factory. The new space has greatly enhanced the Martin experience for the thousands of annual visitors.

As visitors come into Martin's front entrance, they walk across a headstock and fingerboard, through guitar-friendly automatic doors, into a Dreadnought-shaped lobby.

Claire Frances Martin is no stranger to the guitar. From a very early age she has been exposed to the instrument, making it highly likely that she will play a significant role in the future of the company. The April 2008 issue of *Inc. Magazine* introduced Claire to the business world. Above right, Chris and Diane Martin are seen with their daughter, Claire (another C.F. Martin), who was born in 2004 and represents the seventh generation of the Martin family in America. Below, Chris Martin takes Claire on a factory tour to learn the finer points of neck shaping.

In 2011, all of the employees donned their Martin T-shirts and went downstairs to the raw wood processing area for a group photograph. At the time, there were more than 500 employees. Martin's photographer John Sterling Ruth perched himself high up on a stack of mahogany and took this shot. Now, Martin has grown further to more than 600 people, all members of a unique company culture and family-run business that grew from the vision of one man more that 180 years ago. They are all honored to be a part of it.

Martin & Co
EST. 1833

Visit us at
arcadiapublishing.com

Printed in the USA
CPSIA information can be obtained
at www.ICGtesting.com
LVHW070757241223
767241LV00009B/898